Mines

of

Death Valley

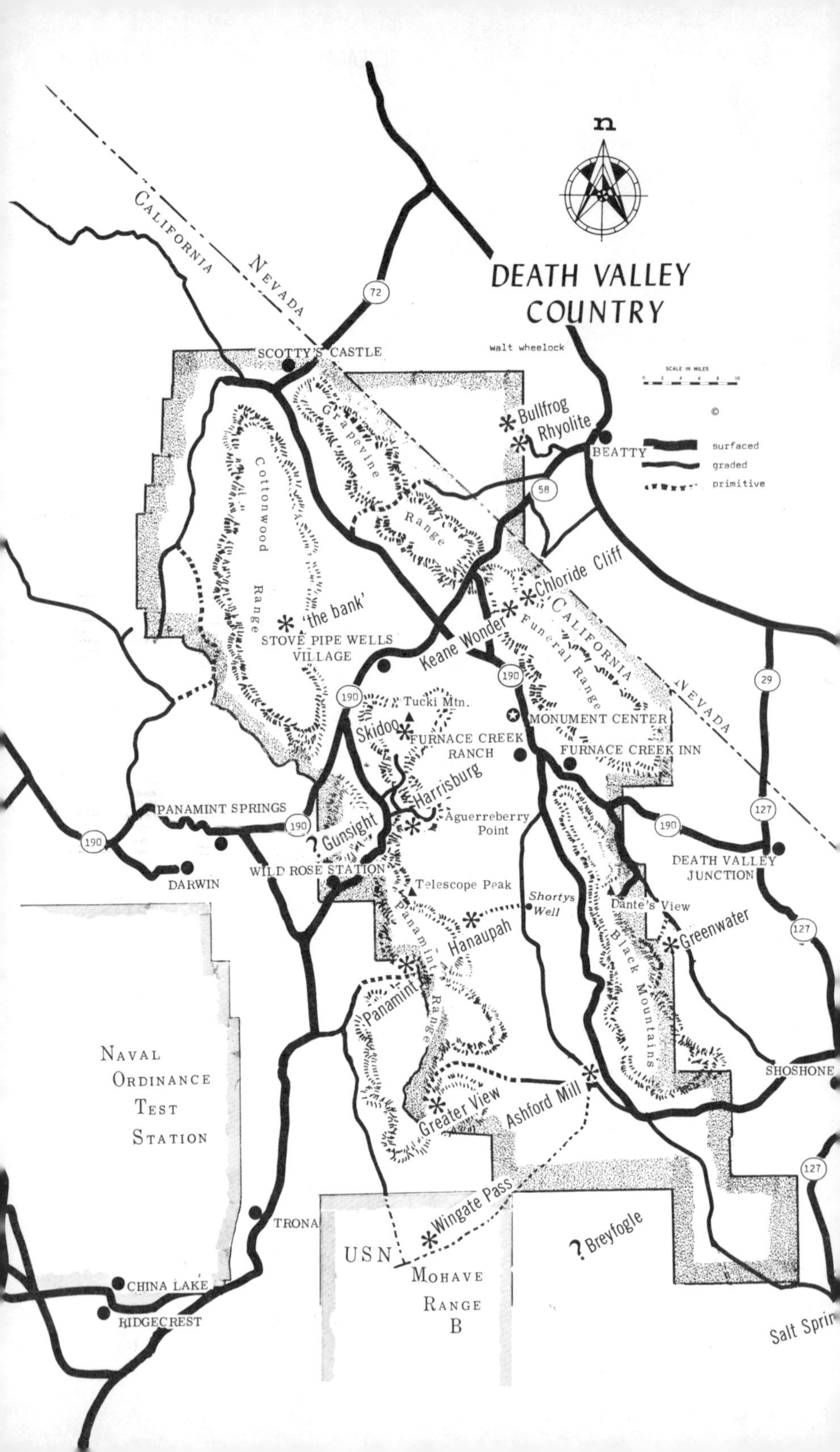
DEATH VALLEY COUNTRY
walt wheelock
n
SCALE IN MILES
surfaced
graded
primitive
CALIFORNIA
NEVADA
72
SCOTTY'S CASTLE
Grapevine Range
Cottonwood Range
Bullfrog
Rhyolite
BEATTY
58
Chloride Cliff
'the bank'
STOVE PIPE WELLS VILLAGE
Keane Wonder
Funeral Range
190
29
Tucki Mtn.
Skidoo
FURNACE CREEK RANCH
MONUMENT CENTER
FURNACE CREEK INN
Harrisburg
PANAMINT SPRINGS
Gunsight
Aguerreberry Point
127
DEATH VALLEY JUNCTION
DARWIN
WILD ROSE STATION
Telescope Peak
Shortys Well
Dante's View
Greenwater
Hanaupah
Panamint Range
Black Mountains
Panamint
NAVAL ORDNANCE TEST STATION
SHOSHONE
Greater View
Ashford Mill
Wingate Pass
TRONA
Breyfogle
USN
MOHAVE RANGE B
CHINA LAKE
RIDGECREST
Salt Sprin

MINES
of
DEATH VALLEY

by
L. Burr Belden

revised edition

La Siesta Press
GLENDALE, CALIFORNIA
1976

related La Siesta publications—

Mary DeDecker
MINES OF THE EASTERN SIERRA

Ronald Dean Miller
MINES OF THE MOJAVE

Roger Mitchell
DEATH VALLEY JEEP TRAILS
INYO-MONO JEEP TRAILS

Walt Wheelock
DESERT PEAKS GUIDE II [Death Valley Country

LA SIESTA PRESS
Box 406
Glendale, California, 91209
PRINTED IN U. S. A.

Contents

Foreword to Revision

Since MINES OF DEATH VALLEY was first published a decade ago, there have been several changes in the Monument — some good and some very bad.

An important item, from the historian's viewpoint, is the project to restore Harmony Borax Works, near the Visitor's Center. Sparked and partially financed by the Death Valley '49ers, this provides an interpretative center of borax history.

When Death Valley was first made a national monument, an exception was made to allow prospecting and mining to continue within its borders. Undoubtedly Congress had in mind the one-jackass miner, who prowled and prospected. He dug with a pick and shovel, and the "gopher holes" he dug, had little impact on the land.

The last important mining in the valley was for borax, but when kernite (sodium borate) was discovered near Mojave, it marked an end to borax in Death Valley. Not only was kernite easier to process, but it was closer to the markets. However, with the development of fiber-glass, colmanite was again in demand. Tenneco Corp. opened a huge open-pit operation in Furnace Creek Wash, near Ryan. In no time, vast tailing piles appeared on the hillsides. But this was not enough. Claim markers appeared around Zabriskie Point, one of Death Valley's most scenic outlooks. Tenneco asked for a permit for a mine a short distance from Dante's View, the famous overlook. This was too much, and TV camera crews filmed Tenneco's rape of Death Valley. Bills were introduced in Congress, to control or eliminate mining in Death Valley.

As we go to press, Congessional activity continues, but no firm decisions have been reached. We can only pray that Death Valley will be protected and saved for future generations.

Walt Wheelock
June, 1976

Introduction

it started in 1849

GOLD, a paying vein that has continued to yield for 115 years, was found on California's Mojave Desert in 1849 some 450 miles from the celebrated Coloma discovery of John Marshall. Simultaneously, in the same region a piece of silver float triggered the initial prospector rush to Death Valley — the land with the forbidding name.

Between the Argonauts of 1849 and the last years of filings during World War II, thousands of single-blanket jackass prospectors and their burros picked and kicked at uncounted rock formations from Cave Springs north to Oriental Wash and from Ash Meadows west to Panamint Valley.

Some struck it rich. More failed. All gave their bit to the writing of one of the West's most fabulous chapters of history. Today, ruins of mills, rusted dump cars and sagging headframes faithfully mark the spots of yesteryear bonanzas.

It is not our purpose to chronicle the troy weight of bullion recovered from the *World Beater*, the *Tizzie* or the *Dublin Colleen*. Rather the writer seeks to reveal the human side of this ever-optimistic breed of rainbow chasers, and preserve for today and tomorrow a bit of the 'you were there' feeling that must come from learning of the doings and adventures of these all-but-forgotten men.

This might be rightly termed a story it has taken 43 years to compile, for the writer's first Death Valley trip was back in 1923 when he heard some of the 'impossible but true' accounts of how the area's mines and boom camps originated. A mule strays — its owner finds the critter chomping grass over a rich outcropping. A weary traveler beds down but can't sleep because a rock keeps punching his back. Morning discloses a fine gold vein. Stage robbers hide out from the law in a remote canyon, and find themselves millionaires when pecking at rocks for amusement. A prospector picks up a likely looking piece of float and then spends half a day squinting around

KEANE WONDER

INCORPORATED UNDER THE LAWS OF THE TERRITORY OF ARIZONA

CAPITAL STOCK $1,500,000 | NON-ASSESSABLE | 1,500,000 SHARES $1.00 EACH

NUMBER 7262 | SHARES

Keane Wonder Mining Company

MINE, SOUTH BULLFROG DISTRICT

DEATH VALLEY, INYO COUNTY, CALIFORNIA

SUPERINTENDENT'S OFFICE, BEATTY, BULLFROG DISTRICT, NEVADA

This Certifies *that* A. Y. Wright Trustee *is the owner of*

Shares of the Capital Stock of

KEANE WONDER MINING COMPANY

transferable only on the books of the Corporation by the holder hereof in person or by Attorney, upon surrender of this Certificate properly endorsed.

In Witness Whereof, *the said Corporation has caused this Certificate to be signed by its duly authorized officers and to be sealed with the Seal of the Corporation*

this 21st *day of* January A. D. 1907

M. Elgar, SECRETARY | Homer Wilson, PRESIDENT

SHARES $1.00 EACH

from Robert Greenawalt collection-to find correctly its true source. Another becomes intrigued with an abandoned Indian camp only to find a rich silver-lead vein. Green-stained rocks around a mountain spring lead to the discovery of copper ore. A party of travelers gets lost when clouds drop so low they obliterate a mountain trail. Dawn reveals scores of gold-bearing rocks bordering their blankets.

Such oddities are true stories that tell the start of famous strikes in the Death Valley region, stories recounted over the years by members of the dwindling fraternity of pack-and-pick men who grubbed at Skidoo, sank shafts at Harrisburg and lived it up at Ballarat.

All photos not credited are from the author's collection.

Walt Wheelock

Salt Spring
the first mine

THE OLD SPANISH TRAIL, a pack train route connecting the northern Mexican outposts of Santa Fe and Los Angeles, was opened in the 1830's. Based, in part, on the earlier explorations of Father Garcés at the west, and Escalante at the east, this route described a vast irregular arc with an apex far up in Utah. A more direct westerly extension of the famed Santa Fe Trail was desired, but blocked, temporarily, by Indian hostility in northern Arizona. Simultaneously, with the Mexican War of 1846 which saw the United States taking what approximates the present states of New Mexico, Arizona, California, Nevada and Utah, the Latter Day Saints – followers of the teachings of Joseph Smith – were driven from their 'Zion' at Nauvoo, Illinois, and under the leadership of Brigham Young headed west for an undecided location remote enough to escape religious persecution.

While en route west this deeply religious migration was visited by United States Army representatives who sought to enlist a battalion of volunteers for war service. President Young of the church saw the occasion as an opportunity both to achieve an informal armistice with the government and to relieve the great financial burden of the migration. The battalion was formed and headed toward Santa Fe. Then it was divided – with the less physically fit turning to join the church's migration while the others, under command of Lt. Col. Philip St. George Cooke headed for California and broke out a crude wagon road in the process. Arriving after the Navy, under Commodore Robert F. Stockton had rescued Gen. Stephen W. Kearny from his mauling at San Pascual, the Mormon Battalion did garrison duty, erected Fort Moore in Los Angeles, guarded the Cajon Pass against Walkara's horse raiders, and even aided Col. Isaac Williams harvest crops at Santa Ana del Chino.

When the Mormon soldiers were paid they dutifully turned a tenth, or tithe, of the pay over to the church, and forwarded much of the remainder to their families who had ended their westward trek to found 'Deseret' in the valley of the Great Salt Lake. The church messengers utilized the Old Spanish Trail, and its new branch to Salt Lake, for repeated trips back and forth between Deseret and southern California. As battalion enlistments were nearing their expiration, the Army proposed second hitches for those desiring. Capt. Jefferson Hunt was placed in command of the battalion. He went to Salt Lake City to confer with President Young, and returned with the word that the church needed young men to help build the 'new Zion', and so the battalion was mustered out of service.

The returning soldiers filled a wagon with grape cuttings, seed, fruit, grain, and other supplies. They brought the wagon through Cajon Pass and over the desert, thus proving the Spanish Trail was adaptable to wheeled vehicles.

The year of 1849 witnessed what must have seemed to the settlers in pioneer Salt Lake City as the migration of "half the world" bound for the California gold fields. So heavy was the traffic that there were well-founded fears that food supplies might give out in Deseret before the 1850 harvest. When some 500 Argonauts arrived too late in the season to chance a crossing of the Sierra Nevada before the deep snows of winter, the Mormon leaders proposed that these groups continue their journey by the longer route, the Spanish Trail, which was safe in winter. Captain Hunt had made three trips over the trail, and was available as a guide. The Sand Walking Company was organized and started southwestward.

In the next chapter the dissension in, and the division of this caravan near Enterprise, Utah, is recounted. The dissenters formed the famous ill-fated Death Valley party. The others, who remained with Captain Hunt, continued over the regular trail, arriving in southern California in time for their Christmas dinner at Santa Ana del Chino.

The old trail entered California from Pahrump Valley with a stop at Resting Spring where there was pure water in sufficient abundance to fill casks for the desert ahead. After Resting Spring the trail struck west toward today's Tecopa, then descended the valley of the Amargosa River to its big bend at the southern end of Death Valley. Close to this bend is another oasis with a little pond of brackish water which is named Salt Spring. Beyond, the trail headed through a rough waterless stretch that terminated only when the Mojave River was reached – downstream from today's Daggett. The journada was only broken by one hole of vile water called Bitter Spring. Hunt's caravan halted at Salt Spring to check on equipment. Some of

the members looked around and found some gold bearing rock on the hill beside the little lake. Then the caravan moved on.

In Los Angeles the gold samples were exhibited and plans were made for some of the men to go back and start mining. That was in January 1850. The Salt Spring gold deposit and other gold veins in the Avawatz Mtns. nearby got onto early maps as 'Mormon Diggins'. Later writers, as is so often the case when remote areas are concerned, changed Mormon Diggins to 'Lost Mormon Diggins.' There is nothing lost about the gold at Salt Spring. It has been mined almost continuously for 115 years.

One of the famous Sublette brothers, Andrew, served as foreman of this mine in the 1850's after an earlier career in the fur trade and the Oregon Battalion.

The original finder of the Salt Spring gold was a Mr. Roan, according to Sublette, who went to the mine in 1851 to represent the Los Angeles Mining Co., of which Benjamin D. Wilson was a founder along with Colonel Williams. The ore was rich but the location too remote to be attractive. A second mining company, having a claim nearby, was the Desert Mining Co. with James F. Hibbard as president. Operating costs were high because of the long hauls. The company was forced to the wall late that summer.

In November of the same year Benjamin D. Wilson formed the Salt Spring Mining Co., taking over the claims of the two rival companies. It became an on-and-off operation, frequently plagued by visits of food-begging Indians.

In the early days of the Civil War Major James H. Carleton established redoubts at both Bitter Spring and Resting Spring. Things became more peaceful. Then the California volunteers ceased patrolling the trail with the war's end. Paiute Indians filtered down from the north to prey on the trail. The Army sent regulars to patrol the Old Government Road to the south but forgot about the outposts along the Salt Lake Trail. A year after Appomatox seven miners were at Salt Spring. Indians who were camping at Sheep Spring, overlooking the oasis, became threatening. One of the miners slipped out and rode 45 miles to the Army's post at Marl Spring, near today's Kelso, to get help. The soldiers came, but too late. They buried the six miners, who had been slain in the meantime.

In 1880's new machinery was set up by another group of owners, and mucn gold recovered. It was not until 1902, however, that Salt Spring became a bonanza under the ownership of J.B.Osborn of Daggett. Osborn also had the *Gunsight* at

Mine Buildings at Salt Spring

Resting Spring, which was another venerable operation dating back to the 1870's. He also had the *Noonday* mine near Tecopa.

At Salt Spring Osborn hit a pocket of high grade, so rich he recovered $60,000 in a single week. Thus, in 1907, when the Tonopah & Tidewater built north from Ludlow, Osborn conceived the idea of reaching the *Gunsight* and the *Noonday* by rail. He had a route surveyed up the hill from the T&T; it wound around like a snake. Osborn ordered the road built in a near straight line -- reasoning that the ore hauling would be all downhill. On the first trip it was necessary to lock the brakes. This procedure was repeated on each subsequent trip, thus giving the Tecopa RR flat wheeled cars. W.W. 'Wash' Cahill, of the T&T ordered all Tecopa ore reloaded and forbid the use of the flat wheeled cars on T&T rails.

The Tecopa stopped running. In 1942, when Sharpe & Fellows dismantled the T&T for war-needed scrap they tore up the Tecopa as well.

Not even World War II stopped Salt Springs for keeps. In 1960 four miners were working there. Orville Massey, one of the group, pointed out to the writer the old shafts of the 1850's, the graves of the six slain miners, the workings where Osborn got his $60,000 bonanza, and then showed some rich ore then being taken from yet other veins.

The Gunsight
and Gunsighters

THE PARTY of Argonauts who headed down the Old Spanish Trail late in 1849 included a sizable group of dissenters who seceded from Capt. Jefferson Hunt's guidance near Enterprise, Utah, and struck almost due west. En route from Salt Lake to Enterprise a pack train had temporarily joined in with the Sand Walking Co. This train of traders was headed by a man known to the '49ers as Capt. O. K. Smith. Capt. Smith carried a map which purported to show a short cut to the California mines. It was a Fremont map of the period on which "an old mountain man" had traced a short cut as told to him by the Ute chief, Walkara. Walkara was the most celebrated raider among the horsethieves who preyed on California's Mexican rancheros prior to the Mexican War. Walkara had driven off horse herds from ranchos as far north as San Luis Obispo and in so doing had blazed a trail from the Cojo district of Tulare County, through Walker Pass, and across the upper Mojave Desert. Walkara had described landmarks as he recalled them. His descriptions had been interpreted as heading west from about Enterprise. In reality Walkara's turnoff appears to have been far south in the Pahrump Valley near Resting Springs.

The Hunt party split, with the majority of the 50 wagons and some 400 men -- electing to follow the horsethief's map rather than continue under the leadership of their guide who was making what was at least his third trip over the route. Gold fever does strange things to men's reason. The Walkara short cut was neither a road nor a trail. Captain Hunt declared it would lead "straight to hell." He was quite right. It led into the middle of Death Valley. Long before Death Valley was reached the seceding party started to fall apart at the seams. On the banks of Beaver Dam Wash several turned south to rejoin the Hunt leadership. Captain Smith promptly forgot his 'followers', who were at a loss to get their wagons across the wash, and he nonchalantly disappeared to the west.

As they were able the stranded Argonauts followed the Smith tracks. After days of rough going the lost gold seekers emerged from Forty Mile Canyon on the desert north of Ash Meadows. They split into clans. These clans, or platoons, were the Jayhawkers, the Manly-Bennett-Arcan families, the Mississippians, the Georgians or 'Bug Smashers', and the Earhart-Nusbaumer group. The Rev. J. W. Brier was traveling with his wife and three small sons. He was chaplain of the Mississippians. At the end of Forty Mile Canyon the Brier wagon broke down. Valuables were buried, and the Briers struggled ahead on foot. In the Amargosa Desert, probably south of Big Dune, the Georgians camped and abandoned wagons – backpacking west. At the head of Furnace Creek Canyon, only a mile or two from Death Valley Junction, the Mississippians left their wagons. At this juncture along came the Briers on foot. Ahead were the Manly-Bennett-Arcan, the Jayhawker, and the Earhart-Nusbaumer parties.

Going down Furnace Creek wash the Jayhawkers had turned north to camp on the valley floor south of the present Stove Pipe Wells Hotel. The Manly-Bennett-Arcan party, plus the family of Harry Wade turned south down the valley and camped at what later historians have identified as Tule Spring. The Earhart-Nusbaumer group looked at the desolate valley expanse and pushed south, veering somewhat to the east, then rejoined the Spanish Trail somewhere around today's Tecopa. The Georgians tramped past the Jayhawker camp and continued on their compass course over Tucki Mtn., one of the hardest routes imaginable. The Briers camped with the Jayhawkers. The Mississippians also came but did not tarry. They noted that the Jayhawkers were burning their wagons and using the wood to dry meat of the oxen they butchered.

From the Jayhawker camp, now identified as Burned Wagons Point, the Mississippians cut around the head of the Funeral Range and up Emigrant Wash toward distant Towne Pass. Their group was in charge of Captain Martin -- who deserves to rank as co-discoverer of the pass, along with Captain Towne of the Georgians. Somewhere along the wash between where Stove Pipe Wells resort and the Emigrant Ranger Station now stand a young Mississippian picked up a piece of silver float. He had lost the front sight of his gun; that night he was able to whittle and hammer out a replacement from that float from the wide silver vein.

The next day or two one group of the Jayhawkers overtook the Mississippians and heard about the silver gunsight. By the time the exhausted parties reached Los Angeles six weeks later – this lone gunsight had grown into "a mountain of silver" and therby touched off Death Valley's first boom.

Down in the Panamint Valley, below Wildrose Canyon, the two platoons of Jayhawkers, with the Brier Family, and the Mississippians got together briefly at what they called Horsebones Camp. There the Mississippian displayed his silver gunsight – which by this time had attracted quite a bit of attention. Who was this enterprising young man? None of the diaries or reminiscenses of the '49ers say. He may have been one of the Turner brothers who are known to have been close friends of the Briers. The Briers went to Los Angeles. Dr. E. French Darwin told of having talked with the Turner brothers at Tejon Ranch. Most of the Mississippians left Horsebones Camp and headed up Shepherd Canyon over the Argus Range to Walker Pass. That the gunsight maker went to Los Angeles is known from the fact that a gunsmith named John Goler replaced it there -- and promptly closed shop to head for Death Valley. The Turners are believed to have gone back for a second helping, also.

Panamint
senators rescue bandits

EARLY in 1873 a group of four or five bandits hauled some bullion they had taken from a Wells Fargo express box into Surprise Canyon in the Panamint Range. They were certain of pursuit but reasoned rightly that neither a sense of duty nor the posted rewards would bring venturesome law officers up the steep, winding canyon where an ambush was possible at every turn. The highwaymen had a supply of provisions. They were sure that the hot breath of pursuit would cool after a bit, or be diverted to some fresher crime.

Needless to say there was not much in the way of diversion in Surprise Canyon. The 'first settlers' amused themselves by more or less aimlessly pecking at the rock walls. Imagine their feelings when these aimless peckings revealed a ledge of almost pure silver "wide enough to drive a wagon through." They had found a second Virginia City, they thought. But what good did it do to own a million if they were unable to go outside and spend it? The only answer was to pay off Wells Fargo; that would require a go-between, and a good one.

Neighboring Nevada had a spectacular senator, one William M. Stewart, who was known throughout the West both as a fighter and a great silver backer. By chance one of the robbers knew Stewart and, fortunately, he seemed to have been unknown to the express company. At least his name had not appeared on the reward posters. Taking several samples of the ore in his saddlebags this robber-turned-mine-owner, rode north to the Comstock Lode where he contacted the senator. The senator agreed, and would find out what the express company wanted as a settlement of the whole affair. The senator's price would be an interest in the mines, plus an interest for his colleague, Senator John P. Jones. Jones, incidentally, had been attracted by the Panamint ore when some of it had been displayed a few weeks earlier by a promoter known as Colonel Raines -- who had tried, without success, to do just what Senator Stewart had agreed to do. The shares of the two senators meant quite a bite in the prospective fortune – but from the bandits' viewpoint it was still a bargain.

Senator Stewart arranged to pay off Wells Fargo. By April, Panamint claims were being filed. Original locators were W. L. Kennedy, R. B. Stewart, and R. C. Jacobs. The publisher at Bishop, W. A. Chalfant, who dug up the location notices had no idea whether or not the trio were members of the hiding banditti. In fact, he surmised assumed names might have been used – names the men adopted at the time of their 'reformation'. Senator Stewart himself is silent on the point in his autobiography published more than 30 years later.

Road-making and milling machinery followed the filing of the claims. Additional prospecting brought other strikes with several more claims recorded in June. Indians were hired as woodcutters and charcoal kilns were erected (not the famous kilns in Wildrose Canyon). Not even two senators could induce Wells Fargo to run a stage line into Panamint. The express company wanted to keep the boom camp's first citizens safe from temptation.

A stage and mail service was a necessity, however. Senator Stewart went to San Bernardino, where with a down payment of bullion as heavy as he could lift to the counter, he obtained the promise of Caesar Myerstein to run the line. The Myerstein Brothers were general merchants and did considerable desert freighting, running wagons as far as Salt Lake City. It was agreed that the stage would make weekly trips. When it was found that the sandy route took two weeks to traverse, it meant extra rigs. The stage left San Bernardino, crossed Cajon Pass over Brown's Toll Road, followed the Mojave River from the Verde Ranch down to the present Helendale, then cut north to Harper Lake, where Black's Ranch served as a supply point and depot. With fresh horses -- the route went north up Black Canyon, past Granite Wells, through lower Panamint Valley and on to a spring near the site of Ballarat. From the spring the line turned east for the last leg up Surprise Canyon.

Not all of Panamint's residents appear to have made peace with the law, or there may well have been some new arrivals. At any rate the spring in north Panamint Valley, the one near the site of Ballarat, received the name 'Postoffice Spring', and for good reason. When the stage driver received a letter addressed to John Doe at Postoffice Spring, he simply dropped it off and hung a rag on a nearby creosote bush. The spring was out on the flat with no screened approaches. A hiding bandit could thus get his mail in safety.

Panamint boomed. The mine owners envisioned a bonanza that held values with depth. Senator Stewart, himself, became so optimistic he promoted the Los Angeles and Independence Railroad — by way of Panamint, of course. The road was actually built and operated between Santa Monica and Los Angeles. It was surveyed to San Bernardino and on up over Cajon Pass. Atop the West Cajon, competition was encountered in the form of surveyors for the Southern Pacific which was then planning its line east to run from the Tehachapi to the Cajon, effectively relegating Los Angeles to the sidelines. The rival survey crews exchanged shots; but the SP men didn't know that the LA&I had a big grading crew at work only a mile or so away. The firing brought the LA&I reinforcements on the run — a roaring blast answered the few scattered SP shots. The Southern Pacific surveyors wisely retreated.

After the Cajon Pass repulse, the SP listened to a subsidy offered by Los Angeles County and built over their present route. The LA&I never did build east beyond Los Angeles. Years later the line was bought by the Southern Pacific; the assets, of course, included the right-of-way over West Cajon. Now, 90 years later, the SP is building a line between Colton and Palmdale, but it is to parallel the Santa Fe through East Cajon rather than follow the old right-of-way. There is a good reason -- the East Cajon summit is more than 1000 feet lower.

Stores, saloons, boarding houses, the Bank of Panamint, and a newspaper all blossomed in Surprise Canyon — a canyon so narrow that there could be no back streets. The main one was over a mile long. Twice the town was destroyed by flash floods that also wiped out the road. T. S. Harris moved his Panamint News to Darwin shortly after the great July 4, 1875 celebration. U.S. Senator George Hearst was developing Modoc across Panamint Valley in the Argus Range. Nearby Lookout and Darwin itself were booming. Panamint values held, but its rock became harder with depth -- and blunted the miners' tools. Gradually the camp creaked to a close. High silver prices have brought brief subsequent revivals -- one of the latest being foiled when the newly rebuilt road washed out once again.

Panamint mill owners just didn't trust bandits. When the mill boss was tipped off that a bunch was waiting to hijack the monthly cleanup he had the silver cast in cannon balls weighing some 700 pounds apiece. The holdup came off on schedule. The bandits tried in vain to heft a cannon ball. They rode off cussing the "dirty mine owners who wouldn't let an honest highwayman make a living."

Breyfogle
Indian captive

WHEN the 'gunsight silver' started the first prospector stampede into the Death Valley region, it but started a precedent — as the wave of silver hunters were dubbed 'Gunsighters'. The Gunsighter who made the biggest splash was a former treasurer of Alameda County, California, who found — and lost — an outcropping of high grade gold to the east of Death Valley. He was Charles Breyfogle.

Breyfogle's find touched off a surge of 'lost mine' hunting that made the earlier Gunsight stampede look like kindergarten stuff. Incidently, it brought the coining of the word 'Breyfogle' which was applied to those seeking his treasure source.

It happened in 1863. More than a century has passed and as many versions of the story have appeared in print as there are intervening years. Breyfogle has been called 'Jake', 'Bill', and 'Sam'. The scene of his find has been 'located' all the way between Goldfield and Las Vegas.

Here, in capsule, are the known facts based primarily on the 1863 files of the REESE RIVER REVEILLE newspaper published in Austin, Nevada. Breyfogle was keeping a hotel at Genoa, a town south of Austin. One night three men with heavy camping outfits stopped. They kept to themselves, and engaged in earnest conversation. Now and then they consulted a map. Early the next morning they were gone.

It didn't take long for Breyfogle to convince himself that his guests were hot on the trail of the *Lost Gunsight*. Breyfogle hastily assembled an outfit, and started out along the trail of the three men which pointed south down the Great Smoky Valley toward the present Tonopah. He really covered ground. At dark he saw a campfire ahead. Sure enough, his ex-guests were there. Entering the fireside circle Breyfogle asked if, because of Indian danger, would they let him join the prospecting trip instead of hunting alone. He had guessed wrong. His mysterious guests of the night before were not prospectors

— they were Confederate sympathizers who were following the back trails to reach Southern armies in Texas. However, they agreed to let Breyfogle go along with them until they reached the Salt Lake Trail where he could throw in with a passing caravan for protection.

Two or three days later they camped in the Amargosa Valley at a site approximating Shoshone. Breyfogle rolled in his blankets a bit to one side. In the pre-dawn grey he awoke to see and hear Indians smashing the heads of his three companions. Quietly he rolled out into the shadows — just in time — as the savages threw fresh fuel on the fire embers to offer light for the looting then under way. After hiding in a bush or grass clump, Breyfogle got to his feet and ran. There was no time to get either gun or supplies, and no time to put his boots on — he ran with them clutched in his hands. He wandered for hours on the desert, and stopped only when his cut and bleeding feet could stand no more, and then rested behind a rocky ledge.

The next morning it was impossible for him to put his boots on his swollen feet. He found a little spring, and filled his boots as an improvised canteen. The next day and the next Breyfogle wandered over the desert without a vague idea where he was. There were hours and hours of delirium for the starving man. At one point -- he knew not where -- he found an outcropping of rich gold ore. Realizing its value he filled his pants pockets and then resumed his wandering. Finally, he found another spring, and sank down in deep sleep. He was wakened at day by a party of Indians who took him to their camp as a captive. There he was made a slave to collect wood and water for the squaws. Between chores the children took command. They had him get down on all fours and mounted him as a horse. They jabbed his ribs with sticks to make 'horsey' buck. Tiring of this pastime, one older delinquent smashed Breyfogle alongside the head with a length of tree limb. The blow injured both the equalibrium and memory of the prisoner. The Indians reasoned he would die, and gladly sold him to a passing wagon train.

Members of the emigrant train, noting Breyfogle's weakened condition, stopped at the Manse Ranch, a few miles north of Stump Spring, in Pahrump Valley. There Mrs. Yount, wife of the owner, and her daughter, Mrs. Harsha White, nursed Breyfogle back to health. His payment for their kindness was a handful of his rich nuggets. He could not, however, give any clear idea where he had found the ore. The Yount boys drove him around to what they thought might be likely spots — without success.

'Castles' at Dublin City

With returning strength Breyfogle was able to join another passing caravan and eventually returned to the Reese River area – where he showed his remaining nuggets. Other groups fitted up outfits and back they went with Breyfogle trying to guide the way. He could remember – up to a point. On one trip the searchers believed they found the massacre site, and reasoned that Breyfogle's escape route had been through Chicago Canyon which connects the Amargosa Valley with Pahrump Valley near the Pahrump Ranch. That was as close to the treasure as anybody got. For 26 years Breyfogle sought his lost bonanza -- in vain. He headed dozens of search parties that combed the deserts around Goldfield, Lida, Horn Silver, Bullfrog, Leeland, Keane Wonder, Saratoga, Salt Spring, and even down to Sandy and Ivanpah. At least once his companions thought he was bluffing, and left Breyfogle stranded near Bonnie Claire. He wasn't bluffing. The Indian youth's savage treatment had permanently impaired his memory.

The Breyfogle lost bonanza story has appeared in many places; no two versions agree. In 1957 the writer was shown a piece of the original Breyfogle ore by a Mrs. Stella White Fisk, daughter of Mrs. Harsha White, and granddaughter of Mrs. Joseph Yount who had nursed Charles Breyfogle back to health after his ransom and release from the Stump Spring band of Indians. The Yount boys, Mrs. White's brothers, made prospecting something of a vocation in between jobs with the Atlantic and Pacific railroad builders at Fenner. One day they found some ore that matched the Breyfogle samples. It was at *Johnnie*, at the northern end of Pahrump Valley. The *Johnnie* mine proved to be a rich producer; it was worked for a time, and then sold. It had a turbulent subsequent history which included a gun fight when some persons attempted to jump the claim.

The story of Breyfogle's experience and release from Indian captivity appeared as a Sunday historical page in the SUN-TELEGRAM of San Bernardino. A month afterwards a letter came from Richard Dillon, director of the Sutro Library in San Francisco, who furnished the names and addresses of relatives of Breyfogle. Among the latter were Lewis Breyfogle of Chanute, Kansas, and Mrs. Eva Breyfogle Lovelace, of Lakewood, Colorado, who had copied the diary of Breyfogle's 1849 overland trek with his brother, Joshua. Charles settled on the East Bay and became treasurer of Alameda County. A grand jury discovered a fund shortage in the department; Breyfogle was indicted and convicted -- though protesting his innocence. A year later his successor noted a couple of unusual book-keeping entries, both in the same handwriting; he trapped a clerk who confessed, and cleared the convicted former treasurer. Then came an unusual chapter in legal history; the district attorney who had prosecuted Breyfogle, and the judge who had pronounced sentence, asked California's governor to correct an error in justice. Breyfogle was finally pardoned.

Charles Breyfogle then tried to pick up the ends of his interrupted career by buying and running a hotel in Genoa. Later, in between lost bonanza hunts, he helped organize the rich Eureka, Nevada mining district in 1889.

This is the story of the Argonaut who found and lost one of the West's most fabled 'mines', a very human person who now comes down through the years in a clear three-dimensional portrait.

Chloride Cliff
the first road

PERCHED high in the Funeral Mountains, about five miles south of Daylight Pass and near the east boundary of the Death Valley National Monument is a ghost town of picturesquely sagging roofs, a long deserted stone mill foundation, and piles of rubble long since grown over with weeds.

Few visitors to the national monument know about Chloride Cliff, and it would be a banner day if more than a single party should visit the site. The only passable roads, rough and rocky, either lead directly across the Amargosa Desert from the ghost town of Carrera, or head south from Daylight Pass, a short distance east of the California-Nevada boundary.

Despite its isolation and the fact it has received little notice for some 90 years, Chloride Cliff is important. The old camp is even older than Panamint. In fact, it marks the site of one of the first commercially operated mines in the entire Death Valley region. Claims were filed in 1873 and operation is said to have started the following year at that remote location 250 miles from the nearest grocery store. Chloride Cliff gave forth rich ore assaying enough to make profitable that distant operation which in the 1870's was surrounded by parties of marauding Paiute Indians bent on waylaying travelers. The Indians had some justification for being on the warpath. They had just been spanked by soldiers over around Camp Independence, and had been ordered to the Fort Tejon reservation. Many escaped to prey on isolated travelers rather than embrace reservation life. Chloride Cliff must have kept a force big enough and armed well enough to discourage attack. The J. L. Yount family which first settled Pahrump Valley and the famous 'Lost Breyfogle' mine party were each attacked in this same general area within the same decade.

Chloride Cliff's principal claim to fame lies in the fact these pioneer mines of the 1870's built the first road connecting Death Valley with civilization. It was, incidentally, the road used afterward by the Eagle Borax Works in 1882, and by Harmony Borax the year following until Harmony's superintendent J.W.S. Perry hired Charley Bennett to construct the famous Wingate Pass road from Furnace Creek to Mojave, the greatly publicized route of the 20-Mule Teams.

The Chloride Cliff road left what is now the Barstow area and went north. Actually, in its southern reaches it was much the same as the route of the San Bernardino-Panamint stage line. At Pilot Knob, or Granite Wells, the Chloride Cliff road wound east of the peak -- a pass where the bandit Tubrucio Vasquez once kept a rock-walled hideout. Near Goldstone the route went more truly north, past Hidden Springs and Myrick Spring to enter Long Valley about opposite the junction of the Needle Peak Lateral. From Long Valley it descended Wingate Wash, went up the west side of Death Valley, then crossed south of Furnace Creek, ascended Death Valley's eastern side to Beatty Junction. Where the old Keane Wonder Mine road leaves the present highway the original Chloride Cliff trace followed a similar pattern but, of course, continued on to the pioneer mining camp.

It is impossible to follow the old route today. The upper end shows faintly, but has not felt a tire for decades. From the head of Wingate Wash south the old route goes through Mojave Bombing Range B and is, therefore, off-limits

For years students of Death Valley history wondered how Chloride Cliff ever obtained supplies back in the 1870's. Then someone recalled the old Elliot History of San Bernardino County published in 1883. Sure enough the road is mentioned -- even with mileage to landmarks -- some of which are a bit confusing in 1966. In the 1950's researchers for the National Park Service found a long-forgotten crossing of the middle valley, Devil's Golf Course; they figured it might antedate the Harmony Borax road -- sure enough, it does.

Wingate Pass
Scotty fools them all

WALTER SCOTT -- Death Valley Scotty -- became a household word after the record-shattering Los Angeles to Chicago trip of his chartered 'Coyote Special' train in July 1905. The publicity-loving extrovert had come west as a youth to join an older brother Warner, in the Virginia City area, had drifted south on the desert, claimed to have made a single trip on a twenty-mule team borax wagon from Harmony to Mojave as a swamper, and had toured with Buffalo Bill's Wild West Show, and had picked up a bit of coin running an assay office of sorts at Goldfield.

Scotty's special train east was one of the world's greatest publicity stunts. To one and all Scotty had told stories of his famous mine in Death Valley. The Santa Fe was eager to publicize its route as the fastest one east. After the Coyote Special run, the railroad put out an advertising booklet replete with pictures of Scott, his wife Josephine, and of course, the rolling equipment. In the railroad pamphlet it was related that the desert Midas asked about the train possibility, and its price, at Santa Fe's general offices in Los Angeles. When Scotty was told the price would be $10,000 the railroad booklet went on to say that Scott reached into one boot and pulled out $5000 then extracted an equal amount from the other boot. It made good reading, but it didn't happen that way. Nearly 35 years afterwards an author C. B. Glasscock, who had been publisher of the paper at Greenwater in 1906, located the Santa Fe receipt that had been issued Scotty. It was for $5500 -- not $10,000. Payment was by check written by Burdon Gaylord, eastern mining promoter. The Coyote Special with Scotty tossing out silver and gold en route was a publicity gag that surpassed all others.

After his return from the amazing trip Scotty was billed as the star in a San Francisco melodrama titled "Scotty, King of the Desert Mine." It played only one night. The second day found Scotty in jail, arrested on a telegraphic warrant from

Chloride Cliff headframe

Sheriff John C. Ralphs of San Bernardino. The warrant was a sequel to a skirmish, or holdup, in Wingate Wash at the southwest end of Death Valley, a skirmish that became known as "The Battle of Wingate Pass," in which Scotty and eastern capitalist companions were held up by two men Scott had sent ahead for just that purpose.

The holdup pair had instructions to shoot one of Scotty's mules; a wild bullet hit and seriously wounded Scotty's brother Warner. In the excitement Scotty forgot his assumed role, spurred ahead, and shouted, "Stop shooting, you hit one of my men." The easterners, disillusioned, shed their role of the suckers and began prosecution.

One of the men who agreed to ambush Scotty's party, and probably the only survivor of the skirmish, is Bill Keys, miner and long-time companion of Scotty. Keys, now retired, lives on his ranch in Joshua Tree National Monument, where his beautiful desert reservoirs are a favorite camping spot for the youth groups he loves.

In 1954, nearly 50 years after the Wingate incident, Keys broke his silence and told of the 'battle'. One morning this writer's telephone rang. The caller was the editor of WESTWAYS. He asked, "Can you run out to Bill Keys' ranch and get him to tell the true story of the Wingate Pass battle?" Knowing Keys, this seemed a doubtful assignment, for no one had heard him allude to the battle — after which, incidentally, he had been arrested.

Out at the desert ranch, sitting under a sprawling grape arbor the question was posed. "Bill, would you be willing to tell about that Wingate Pass battle in which Indian Bob Belt shot Warner Scott?"

Keys, who had been telling of a new lead he had recently uncovered in his Desert Queen mine, became silent. Then, a smile spread over his face and he said, "Well, I guess the statute of limitations has run out by now, so it won't hurt."

This is the way Bill Keys remembers the battle: When Scotty was in New York he had interested a broker in his 'mine' and obtained a grubstake from Julian Gerard of the Knickerbocker Trust Co. The grubstake, $1500, was to provide Gerard with a half interest in the new and very rich prospect Scotty was developing. After Scotty had made his famous train ride to Chicago, Gerard started writing about the 'mine'. Scott appeared in Riverside with a heavy chain-bound bundle he said contained gold amalgum. Riversiders scarcely raised an eyebrow. Next he went to Philadelphia where he claimed he was robbed while en route to show Gerard the gold. The newspapers quoted Scotty as saying he had lots more, and Gerard seemed satisfied for a time. But then the Gotham banker began to write to get a report on the mine's progress. He wanted a big operation to show people, and probably float stock. Replies from Scotty continued to be optimistic, but patience was wearing thin in Wall Street.

Gerard wrote Scotty that he was coming out to see the mine with his own eyes. Scotty had a camp in Desert Hound Canyon, northeast of where Ashford Mill now stands in Death Valley. On the canyon side he had a prospect hole that showed a fair vein of gold but Scott had never taken the time to open the vein beyond the 10-foot level. A half mile down the canyon Keys had a mine, a good one, which he later sold to Boston capitalists. There was a road up Desert Hound, now re-named Scotty Canyon. It ended at the Keys mine. There was just a mule trail from there up to Scotty's camp.

When Scotty received word that Julian Gerard was coming to Death Valley to see the mine, he was perplexed – but ever the showman, Scotty evolved a plan to give Gerard a taste of the traditional 'wild west', and in so doing – he hoped – cause the banker to lose all taste for Death Valley and its secluded mines. Scotty conferred with Keys, and they planned to fake a holdup and turn around before reaching Death Valley. Keys interposed "Suppose this Gerard doesn't scare and demands to go ahead?" It was agreed that in that case Scotty would show them Keys' mine – passing it off as his own.

In preparation for the Gerard party Scotty polished up a four-mule rig. Harness buckles were nickeled, and the buckboard freshly varnished. Warner Scott and Albert M. Johnson, Chicago insurance magnate whom Scotty introduced as a doctor, went along on horseback.

Keys and an Indian, Bob Belt, started out a day ahead. They were to ride up the old Wingate route to the east end of Long Valley, wait there for the Scott-Gerard party, and then shoot a lead mule of Scotty's team of four. Plans started according to the book, but unknown to Keys, Belt carried whiskey rather than water in one canteen. It was hot up in the rocks bordering Wingate Pass. Also, the Scott caravan was late. By the time it was within gunshot of the 'highwaymen' Belt was so drunk his gun barrel described an arc of 20 degrees. He shot just the same, his bullet hitting Warner Scott in the groin. It was then that Scotty panicked and in so doing, unfortunately, tipped off the easterners.

San Bernardino County Sheriff Ralphs was not a lawman to

To my friend [illegible]
Death Valley Calif 1907
Scott

be trifled with. When the news of the fake holdup reached San Bernardino Ralphs headed north. He wanted Walter Scott, but Scotty had caught a train for San Francisco. Warner was taken to a Los Angeles hospital by Johnson, while the Gerard party chased Keys, who surrendered after first eluding the sheriff. S. W. McNabb, Ralphs' undersheriff and later U. S. District Attorney, went to Los Angeles where he brushed aside guards to personally inspect Warner Scott's wound.

Trial was set in San Bernardino superior court with both the district attorney and sheriff professing an air-tight case. As the trial opened however, the defense introduced a surveyor who testified that the 'battle' scene was actually 440 yards north of the San Bernardino-Inyo County boundary.

That threw the case to Independence, more than 200 miles north in Owens Valley. Inyo's superior court was not to convene for another three months. Gerard and his friends decided they were suckers, after all, and went back to New York. It seemed that there were more important things for the vice-president of the Knickerbocker Trust Co. to do than to prosecute Death Valley Scotty.

So ends the saga of the Battle of Wingate Pass.

Greenwater
and Diamond Lil

EAST of the Black Mountains, between the Shoshone-Ashford Mill road to the south, and the Ryan borax areas to the north, there is an upland mesa bearing the name of Greenwater Valley. The name comes from a highly publicized copper camp which boomed 60 years ago only to fade after the panic of 1907. Greenwater copper stocks were widely sold and eagerly bought on the mining exchanges, much of the eagerness being due to the magic name of Charles M. Schwab, mining and steel tycoon, who was a backer of Greenwater's largest company.

The early 1900's saw the fabulous mining boom in southern Nevada. It started with Tonopah, moved south to Goldfield, branched west to the Lida district, and continued south to Bullfrog. Rhyolite and Gold Center. The Bullfrog discovery came in 1904 and set forth a boom that spawned Rhyolite, one of the most fabulous mining towns. Boomers continued to move on south, even brought life to the almost forgotten Chloride Cliff again, and on to the Greenwater Valley, where some copper ores gave substance to back the dreams and stock sales.

Greenwater was rough — and tough. The desperados who were escorted out of camps farther north landed at Greenwater at the end of the line. Some of these gunmen were so tough that even Greenwater's constable quit. Miners and merchants who wanted a decent chance to survive, got together and chose a huge youngster from Alabama with nerves of steel as the new constable. His name was Charles A. Brown. After facing down a dozen bad men he earned a reputation that caused the lawless tribe to shun the copper camp. It was no surprise to those who knew Charley Brown that he went on to become highway commissioner, county supervisor, and then a powerful senior member of the California senate.

The camp which became Greenwater was not, ironically, the start of the brief boom. The start was at a nearby site named Furnace — for the Furnace Creek Copper Co.

Before the arrival of the Tonopah & Tidewater railroad the bustling copper camp was reached by stage from the Las Vegas & Tonopah over at Ash Meadows. In between the railroad and Salsberry Pass was a way spot known as Fairbanks Ranch. It was a desert station where the traveler bought meals, drink, and feed. The owner was Ralph J. Fairbanks who became the founder of Shoshone and Baker successively. One of the best loved desert men, 'Dad' Fairbanks was a prospector — but above all a humanitarian who rescued dozens of hapless men from the region's searing heat.

The Fairbanks Ranch is a good place to introduce another Greenwater resident whose name invariably comes up when old timers reminisce. The 'chug line' as the stage was called, halted one day at the ranch for lunch. Fairbank's daughter Stella ran to her mother, "Mama, a lady got off the stage and started drinking in the saloon with the men. She is smoking a cigar, too." The 'lady' was the well-known Diamond Lil, proprietor of a house of sinful pleasure in Rhyolite who was on her way to do a different kind of 'prospecting'. Evidently she liked the view at Greenwater, for Lil soon had a place alongside Murphy Brothers store, the post office, the unique Death Valley CHUCKAWALLA office, and several drink emporiums.

Diamond Lil was a larger than average woman, with a wasp waist encased in the tightly laced corset of the day. She had a leopard skin coat and a penchant for wearing it a bit late in the Spring or early in the Fall. She ever flashed a toothy smile in greeting customers as 'dearie'. The reason for the smile was Lil's proudest adornment, a table-cut diamond set in an upper incisor -- which gave her the Diamond Lil trademark. In early Greenwater days she was called 'Diamond Tooth Lil', or just 'Diamond Tooth', but later, at both Silver Lake and Crackerjack, where she and her 'girls' held court, it was just Diamond Lil.

Arthur Kunzie and Frank McAllister filed Greenwater's first copper claims in 1905 but it was not until late that year that ore samples displayed in Barstow brought Joe Harvey, a mining engineer, to the scene. He took more samples and started for Daggett only to be caught in a cloudburst near Cave Springs, in which he lost his outfit and ore samples. What he had seen, however, caused him to backtrack after a second Daggett visit for supplies. The second time he took a span of mules he had freshly shod at Seymour Alf's blacksmith shop. Harvey's second bunch of samples were so good he forwarded them to the mining magnate Patsy Clark. Clark authorized Harvey to buy the claims of Fred Birney and Phil Creaser.

Tasker L. Oddie, later U.S. Senator, F.M. 'Borax' Smith, and Patsy's brother, Senator W.A. Clark came and bought. A big bunch of claims were combined and sold for over $4 million. The Greenwater boom was born with scores of newcomers arriving daily from all points of the compass.

Bonanza finder Frank 'Shorty' Harris appears elsewhere in this book. He had staked out a bunch of Greenwater claims and given them to Judge Decker at Rhyolite. The judge left for Independence but his cruise ship got stuck on a bar in Rhyolite — the claims were never recorded.

How long Greenwater could have remained a siren for stock sale money is a guess. When the bottom dropped from mining stocks Greenwater became deserted, deserted by all but two. Fairbanks stayed on – moving buildings to the new town of Shoshone he was building at an old Indian campsite along the Tonopah & Tidewater. Charley Brown, the husky young constable, stayed too, as Fairbanks' helper. He became a partner of Fairbanks, and married the latter's daughter Stella, and almost singlehandedly reared a modern community astride a state highway he promoted. Today it is hard to find even the site of Greenwater, but Shoshone is the metropolis of eastern Inyo.

What happened to Diamond Lil? Glasscock, who was a partner in both the GREENWATER TIMES and the CHUCKAWALLA related Lil's departure. It seems that when the newspaper partners had urgent business in Rhyolite one week they left one Billy Robinson to put out the paper. Billy undoubtedly thought it funny when he swiped a high society ball item from a New York paper and made it a local item by substituting names of the more proper Greenwater matrons. The wives saw no humor in being libeled thusly and depicted in opera gowns. Their husbands took up the cause. Billy was tried and actually sentenced to hanging. He escaped, and hid in Lil's house. Lil knew full well that the matrons and social arbiters had no use for her either. She hitched up, put Billy on the buggy seat beside her and headed back for Rhyolite.

Charley Brown at Greenwater

Bullfrog

Shorty liked to talk

ED L. CROSS and Frank 'Shorty' Harris had their bedrolls spread at the *Keane Wonder* mine, south of Daylight Pass in the summer of 1904. Both were out prospecting. According to the expression that still persisted after nearly 40 years, they were 'breyfogling' Despite the season, neither thought of going 'outside' to a cooler spot though Ed had a home over in Lone Pine. Harris had been prospecting around southern Nevada and the Death Valley region for over a decade. He had reached both Tonopah and Goldfield just a bit too late to get in on the good claims. Shorty also had missed the better stuff that was found around the *Keane Wonder.*

It is difficult to picture two more different men than these two who teamed up to discover the Bullfrog mine in Rhyolite Hills. Harris, aptly named for his under-length legs, ever talkative and jumping about; Cross tall, spare, and soft-spoken. It was this writer's great privilege to have interviewed each of the co-discoverers.

The Bullfrog claim sold at a good figure. It should have been, for it touched off a rush equal or superior to that at Goldfield. Shorty took most of his pay in whiskey. Ed pocketed his and bought a ranch down in Hemet Valley where he lived until the late 1950's.

Cross and Harris moved out from the *Keane Wonder* on the morning of August 9, 1904 headed for a blowout in the hills to the north that Harris had seen on an earlier trip. Out in the flat, about where the Death Valley - Beatty road is located, Harris picked up a piece of greenish float. It was flecked with gold. He called Cross – and they found other gold-bearing pieces of quartz. Harris turned his rock over and over. From every angle he could see gold flecks. He exclaimed, "Ed, that rock just lays in my hand and squints at me like a green bull-frog."

The prospectors peered about – doing some squinting of their own, then decided to look toward the hills for the lode.

Late that afternoon they found the mother vein, and camped. The next day they made out location notices. Ed hurried away to file them. Not too certain of county lines, he filed in both Esmeralda and Nye counties. Shorty moved about — doing what he could do best — publicizing the strike as the "biggest thing yet." Soon the stampede was on from the Nevada camps. Bob Montgomery staked out the *Montgomery-Shoshone* some three or four miles away. His first ore ran $500 a ton. He turned down a cool $1 million for it. The Bursch brothers came and laid out the townsite of Rhyolite near the Montgomery mine. Walter Beatty, his Indian wife and family lived at nearby Beatty Springs. Beatty sold the spring water for more money than he believed existed — and it was piped to Rhyolite. Beatty started a town on his homestead, south of the springs. A rag town at first, it grew into a commercial center. Beatty was named the first postmaster, a job he was forced to relinquish when a nosey government man came along and found that Beatty could not read nor write. His successor was a young storekeeper, R.A. Gibson, who had set up business with a load of lumber, hay, and other provisions he had trucked up from far off Ivanpah by Rose & Palmer.

Tasker L. Oddie, Tonopah's fearless sheriff, arrived and organized the Bullfrog Mining Co. One of the directors was Key Pittman, who years later was Oddie's colleague in the senate.

Bullfrog, the discovery town, continued to grow — but Rhyolite did so in a more spectacular way. It boasted a Jay Cook Bank housed in a three-story concrete and steel building, the one whose ruined facade delights so many present day photographers. Rhyolite had a whole street of stone and concrete structures. Bullfrog had one of the finest and strongest jails in the whole state. It is still there.

In the big names of mining, Charles M. Schwab, Senator W. A. Clark, and Malcolm Macdonald came — and invested. Rhyolite boasted not only piped water — it had an ice plant and a brewery — in addition to its numerous mercantile houses, saloons, and what have you.

Senator Clark and F.N. 'Borax' Smith were rivals in bringing railroads. They started as partners with Smith starting rails from Clark's San Pedro, Los Angeles & Salt Lake at the Nevada siding named Las Vegas. Then, while Clark was vacationing in Europe, he read more and more about the Bullfrog boom. He decided to make the feeder line a Clark one. Of course, that didn't suit Smith, the borax king — who thought he had a firm commitment to build from Las Vegas to his big borax mine, the *Lila C,* near the present Death Valley Junction. When Clark returned from Europe, Smith's crews were already 22 miles on their way from Las Vegas toward the *Lila C.* A Clark attorney came out, and in effect read Clarence Rasor and John Ryan, Smith's surveyor and superintendent, the riot act. They were ordered to cease and desist, and very plainly told they could not connect with the Clark railroad at Las Vegas or any other point. The Clark and Smith agreement had been a verbal one – reached over dinner at San Francisco's Palace Hotel.

The infuriated Smith announced he would never ship a pound of borax over Clark's railroad. He went further – he moved his construction crews to Ludlow, 55 miles east of Barstow – on the Santa Fe, and even before the survey could be completed was laying ties and rails toward the north, over Brownwell Palya and on toward Soda Lake. Smith announced his railroad, the Tonopah and Tidewater would, as its name implied, give a tidewater outlet to Nevada's mines. In practice, however, he was happy over the Santa Fe junction at Ludlow for his southern terminal. Smith's T&T was held up by heavy construction in Amargosa Canyon, the canyon of hanging rocks, and reached the Bullfrog area after Clark's Las Vegas & Tonopah – which had both a shorter and an easier route. Then, the LV & T erected a magnificent station at Rhyolite, one that has been preserved long after the tracks were gone. A third railroad also entered the picture, the Bullfrog & Goldfield, a little line which was to all purposes, save ownership, a southern extention of the existing Tonopah & Goldfield. LV&T extended its tracks north to Goldfield, but the T&T was content with a B&G junction. Now all three lines are but memories. T&T, the last to go, was torn up in 1942 to furnish iron for the war effort – which action, incidentally had been opposed by its owners – Pacific Coast Borax. During the boom years the mining railroads had been big money earners. The first months after the T&T was completed solid pullman trains ran from Tonopah to Los Angeles and back each weekend.

While the railroads were coming, the southern Nevada towns were on the downgrade. After the B&G and LV&T dropped out, the T&T picked up the big Rhyolite depot which served as an admirable terminal for the trains hauling the suckers to C.C. Julian's gyp excursions to his highly touted Leadfield in 1926.

There was rivalry between Beatty and Rhyolite. Beatty sought to corral the travelers. It built the Montgomery Hotel. The Montgomery was not at all modest in advertising it had the only bath in Nevada south of Goldfield. It was true. What passed for a hotel in Las Vegas was just a big tent fronting the tracks. But Rhyolite raised the ante and advertised its new Southern Hotel had TWO baths. This was really catering to the carriage trade.

At the end of 1906 Rhyolite had 10,000 people, if the 'residents for a day' were counted. Not even a reservation would assure one a bed unless the hotel clerk was given his tip. The profits to merchants were almost as big as those going to the mine promoters. The Porter Brothers of Randsburg took 18 wagonloads from their stock, moved it across Death Valley – selling half the supplies by the time their long caravan was unloaded. A poor lunch counter had a line so long it took an hour to get served. It was no town for a prohibitionist. Even the coffee smelled and tasted of liquor. The beaneries kept their water in whiskey barrels.

The RHYOLITE HERALD appeared in 1905. It had competition in the BULLFROG MINER and the RHYOLITE BULLETIN along with the DEATH VALLEY MAGAZINE, which was a monthly. There is a copy of the latter down in the Death Valley Museum now. Its inside cover is devoted to a preview of the next issue and announcing the feature article would be by Col. John B. Colton who was to tell of his crossing Death Valley in 1849 with the Jayhawkers. Despite the fact that references to the Colton article have appeared in many of the bibliographies, don't take the trouble to look for it. It never existed. When the next month rolled around the DEATH VALLEY MAGAZINE had a sign on its front door: "Gone to Rawhide."

Over to the west of the business district of Rhyolite there is the shell of a large concrete building. It was the schoolhouse built with a $20,000 bond issue in the Fall of 1907. Rhyolite had 270 school-age kids the previous June; by the time the new building was ready there were only enough left for classes in a single room.

Today Rhyolite and Bullfrog are ghost towns, towns easy to reach for winter tourists. Rhyolite has imposing ruins – a museum or two, and the famous L. J. Murphy bottle house. Two or three houses are occupied, and the old timers like to show visitors where millionaires of the day hung out. The *Montgomery-Shoshone* is certain to be high on the list and the visitor will likely be told that it was discovered by an old Indian named Johnnie, who gave it to E. A. 'Bob' Montgomery in trade for a pair of overalls. It is a good yarn, but it isn't so. Montgomery found his own mine. Those who prefer truth to fiction owe a debt to Harold Weight of Twentynine Palms who published a book entitled, "Rhyolite, Death Valley's City of Golden

Dreams." Weight dug up an early copy of the INYO REGISTER Bill Chalfant's paper over in Bishop; it gives a true story of the *Montgomery - Shoshone* discovery as printed before the Indian and overalls yarn was invented.

In the Fall of 1957 the writer called on Ed Cross at his daughter's home in Hemet, and with the retired mine owner checked over salient facts in the story of Bullfrog and Rhyolite. In parting the aged man was asked, "Mr. Cross, how is it that so much has been written about Shorty Harris at Bullfrog, and so little about you?"

Cross laughed and said, "Shorty liked to talk."

WORKING A CLAIM.

Ruins of Cook's Bank, Rhyolite

Skidoo

he was hanged twice

SKIDOO, a mining camp perched high on the northern brow of the Panamints where it overlooks the famous Stovepipe Wells sand dunes, has been known far and wide as "the town that had the hanging." Perhaps this is none too fair a distinction. Today, Skidoo is a small collection of buildings, one of which housed the bank and general store, one the mill, while others served as miner's cabins. One or two old-timers may be found occupying one of the remaining cabins, and picking over the veins for high grade.

Fifty-five years ago things were different in Skidoo. The camp boasted a post office, a bank, a phone line that stretched all the way across Death Valley to Rhyolite, a weekly newspaper known as the SKIDOO NEWS, general store, lumber yard, blacksmith shop, several saloons, and running water piped all the way from Telescope Peak -- 23 miles distant. It was the 23-mile water line which gave Skidoo its name for the slang expression of the day was 'Twenty-three Skidoo'. Skidoo meant scram - vamoose —

Skidoo's most famous incident, the lynching of a drunken saloon keeper, Joe 'Hooch' Simpson, on a night in April 1908 made Skidoo the most advertised mining camp in the West. Perhaps it was not just the lynching itself but the congeniality of the Skidoo-ites that brought the wave of publicity, for 24 hours after Simpson had been interred on boot hill, a Los Angeles HERALD reporter arrived. He had come all the way from Lone Pine in a livery rig to get the story about the hanging. Skidoo folk were right proud of such notice and promptly set out to show their appreciation. They disinterred Simpson's corpse and hanged it a second time just so the reporter could take a picture.

The editor of the SKIDOO NEWS chronicled his big scoop in the issue of April 5, a copy of which has, fortunately, been preserved in the Inyo County Library at Independence. The headlines read:

"MURDER IN CAMP. Murderer Lynched with General Approval. Joe Simpson shoots Jim Arnold dead and is hanged by citizens." Fifty-two years after the lynching, visitors to the Death Valley Encampment were given eye witness accounts of 'Hooch' Simpson's lynching by two of the few onlookers still living. They were George Cook of Lone Pine and Bill Keys of Joshua Tree who spoke at a campfire among the sand dunes. This writer interviewed the pair whose answers to questions were carried by loudspeakers to the hundreds of campfire visitors. Here is a composite of the two stories. Simpson and a partner ran a tent saloon near the big store and bank. One morning business may have been a bit dull so Simpson took to drinking his wares. It was not uncommon, one surmises, for he was universally known as 'Hooch'. It was Sunday morning and Joe was not only drunk, he was drunk and armed. Jim Arnold was the town banker, at what was named the Southern California Bank. Simpson weaved into the bank, pointed his gun and demanded $20. Bystanders overpowered him and took his gun. Joe became abusive and Arnold threw him out.

Three hours later Joe recovered his gun from the stove where his partner had hidden it and went back to the bank. Confronting Arnold again he asked, "Have you got anything against me, Jim?" Arnold answered, "No, Joe, I have nothing against you." "Yes you have," Joe retorted, "prepare to die." With that he shot Arnold near the heart. Then he turned his gun on Joe Macdonald, also of the bank, and would have shot him had not his attention been diverted by a reeling drunk -- Gordon McBain, who though unarmed attempted to arrest Joe. McBain, incidentally, got between Joe and a rifle-aiming physician only 100 feet distant. Bystanders soon disarmed and handcuffed Joe. Arnold died that evening.

Simpson showed no remorse. In fact, he became boastful over his marksmanship. The poker parlor, Club Skidoo, was converted into a temporary guardhouse.

The sheriff was not expected until Thursday; the miners determined that Simpson should pay with his life then and there.

On Wednesday night the guard watching Simpson was overpowered by Skidoo vigilantes. The prisoner was taken outside and hanged to a telephone pole. The next day, Thursday, Judge Thisse conducted an inquest.

The SKIDOO NEWS remarked on how quietly the lynching had been conducted. A joker had told the drunken McBain that he was to be a second victim. McBain promptly left camp.

The NEWS editor remarked that McBain's running from imaginary pursuers made more noise than the hanging.

On Friday the Los Angeles reporter arrived. The second hanging was decorously staged with a tent frame, a far less public spot than the telephone pole. The Skidoo editor closed his full page coverage with a bit of moralizing about the stoutness of the town's telephone poles -- which he opined should stand as a warning to evil-doers.

Oh, yes. The coroner's inquest found Simpson had died of strangulation at the hands of persons unknown.

In April 1908 Keys was mining in Skidoo. Cook was hauling supplies back and forth to Rhyolite. At the Death Valley campfire on Nov. 10, 1960 Cook and Keys met each other for the first time in nearly 50 years. Around the fire Cook admitted he was one of the two men who went inside the guardhouse and hauled Simpson outside -- turning him over to the vigilantes. Keys recalled that there was a crowd of 60 men surrounding the tent of Constable Sellers when Simpson had been moved.

Skidoo has been dormant for many years. The famous water line was hauled away during World War I. There is plenty of ore left but it is no longer lying loose on the ground as it was one foggy night in 1906 when Harry Ramsey and 'One Eye' Thompson became lost on a trip from Furnace Creek to Harrisburg. Having lost the trail they prudently halted and bedded down. Morning revealed promising ore-bearing rocks within arm's reach of their blankets.

Mill at Skidoo

Ashford Mill
the fort

NEARLY 45 miles south of Furnace Creek Inn there is a major Death Valley road intersection where the east and west highways join. Another road heads east via Jubilee and Salsberry passes to Shoshone, while a fourth route goes south to join the state highway at Salt Spring. A bit west of the present junction is a sizable rectangle of massive concrete walls, the abandoned Ashford Mill. Ever since Death Valley National Monument was created in 1933 countless thousands of tourists have asked park rangers, "Who built that fort down south of Badwater, and why?"

Death Valley specializes in the unusual -- and the story of Ashford Mill certainly stands near the top of this category. It happened this way, according to the late Senator Charles A. Brown, who was managing the Fairbanks and Brown establishment at Shoshone when the mill was erected. The Ashford brothers lived in 'Dublin City' in the summer months when it was a bit too warm for Death Valley prospecting. This namesake for Erin's capitol consisted of nothing more than caves dug into a cutbank and fitted with doors and windows, and was a favorite summer camp of the old-timers.

The Ashfords developed a prospect in the Black Mountains, some three miles up the canyon to the northwest of today's road junction. In addition to some spectacular high grade there were broad veins of milling-quality gold. A mill on the spot was the preferred way to mine the ore at a profit. An engineer was consulted, and he proposed a crusher and stamp operation. A test of gravel in nearby Rhodes Wash showed it suitable for the making of concrete. A carload of cement was ordered from Crestmore, 250 miles away by rail. When the cement reached the Shoshone siding of the Tonopah & Tidewater Railroad the Ashfords were surprised to find they had two carloads instead of the one they had ordered.

A telegram was sent to the Riverside Cement Co., advising them of the mistake, and asking for instructions. The cement company figured the freight cost back over the T&T and Santa Fe, and decided it was more than the product was worth to its makers. "Keep it with our compliments", was the answer to the Ashfords.

Alex McLaren was boss of the mill erection. He used a rich four-to-one mix, then used his extra concrete in thickening the walls. It is a safe wager that Ashford Mill will continue to be a Death Valley landmark for a long time. It was built in 1915. Machinery was hauled off during World War II when no piece of metal was safe anywhere on the desert.

The three Ashford brothers were Harry, Henry, and Rudolph. They had located their mine in 1907 and were hauling away picture rock in 1914 when one B.M. McClausland came along. He liked the prospects so well he agreed to pay $100,000 for the mine and the then projected mill. The Ashfords copied what they thought was a printed sales contract they saw in a book. They had no lawyer and in copying the printed form it seems they left out some important words. When it came time to pay -- McClausland refused. The Ashfords sued. After a year the suit was decided against the Ashfords. The mill cost was now on their backs and their debts were so heavy they couldn't operate the big mill. It was closed. For a time the brothers took ore out by wagon, past their idle mill, to have it processed elsewhere. Then the operation ground to a halt.

Bill Keys, whose *Desert Hound* mine was in the next canyon claims there is plenty of untouched ore in the Ashford.

After being forced to the wall by the McClausland suit the Ashfords negotiated a partnership -- headed by a Magyar nobleman, Count V. A. Baranoff, and William Cody, nephew and namesake of 'Buffalo Bill'. Count Baranoff was minus a leg which he said he had lost in a duel. He rather startled desert folk when he appeared at Silver Lake wearing Hapsburg court decorations as an added touch to his prospector's garb.

In mid-summer the count decided he wanted to see 'his mine'. A rig was outfitted at Silver Lake; four days later when the party was unreported, W.H. Brown, the T&T agent, set out on a rescue mission. He found the Baranoff party hopelessly mired. He bundled the occupants into his rig and hurried back to Silver Lake. The nobleman, badly dehydrated, and craving water, sought to supplement his carefully doled-out water with ice he secretly swiped from the bag on his head. He died -- and was buried at Silver Lake. Later his family had the body removed. Since the Baranoff-Cody episode the Ashford mine has been quiet -- but after all, most mines are quiet these days.

Jean Le Moigne
and his bank

JEAN LE MOIGNE, a graduate in engineering and chemistry from a university in France, deserves the title of dean among Death Valley's prospectors. He sought and found ore everywhere from Calico to Pioche, but it was in Death Valley proper that his story begins and it was in the same blistered trough that it reached its tragic end.

The titanic borax chapter of the valley and its environs has no place in this book. A mere chronicle of its high spots would require a sizable volume, but it was borax that brought Jean (the Americans soon knew him as John, and later as 'Cap') to Death Valley and dropped him there alone, and jobless, 5000 miles from home and friends.

Jean was called from Paris by his fellow countryman Isadore Daunet, who headed Death Valley's first borax enterprise, Eagle Borax, in 1882 – a year before William Tell Coleman's larger Harmony Borax started near Furnace Creek. Daunet had trouble refining his cottonball and sent for Jean, the young chemist son of old country friends. Between the time Daunet offered Jean a job, and the time of his arrival, the little Eagle Borax plant went on the rocks. A heartbroken Daunet took his own life.

Eagle had probably been both the simplest and least efficient borax plant devised. It consisted of an open vat which had an Indian-tended fire beneath. Into the vat other Indians dumped cottonball borax they had gathered on the valley floor. After boiling, the solution was drawn off into small tanks where it cooled. The borax crystalized and was harvested. It contained so much foreign material it sold at too low a price to pay expenses.

Very possibly the young chemist would have devised a more efficient operation but he arrived just at the time Eagle Borax folded.

Massive ruins of Ashford Mill

Death Valley was a far different land than Jean Le Moigne had expected; yet despite what must have been an initial forbidding picture, he stayed for 40 years. Along with the news of Daunet's death Le Moigne learned that Eagle Borax was without funds. He had come to Death Valley on advanced funds – but there was no money for a return trip. He turned prospector. The change from brilliant university graduate to 'desert rat' was a complete one, so complete that Le Moigne sonn came to avoid all trappings of civilization, and also to avoid companionship, and show a disdain for money. In the 1890's he is known to have expressed the hope to visit France, but a decade later, when he had profitably sold a mine or two, Le Moigne did not want to leave his desert.

Throughout the 1910-20 decade Le Moigne lived in a rock cabin in the Cottonwood Mtns. The cabin location was in a canyon which now appropriately bears the name 'Lemoin' as near an approximation to Le Moigne as some cartographer could master. A quarter mile upstream from the cabin was Jean's silver mine, the one he called his 'bank'. The mine was a small one, but consisted of a ledge of almost pure silver. He knew the ledge would give out if worked regularly. He did not even sink a shaft – but worked it from a trench, which with depth, he stoped, prefering to handle waste rock twice rather than to install machinery which might tempt him to "overdraw the bank."

Despite his tactiturn disposition, Le Moigne is known to have taken a partner, Bill Stewart. That was in 1916. Bill lived up Emigrant Canyon in a tent while Jean stayed in his rock cabin. The partners were 10 miles apart at bedtime.

Earlier Le Moigne had lived for several years down at Bicycle Lake, now on the Fort Irwin reservation, where he briefly ran a store, and had a house built of lumber hauled from Barstow. When the house burned Le Moigne went back to his cabin in the canyon – close to his 'bank'.

As a storekeeper Le Moigne was something special. He was out prospecting much of the time; he always left the door unlocked. A plate on the counter served as the cash register. Customers served themselves and left what they considered the right price in the plate. Strange thing is, the system seemed to work. That was, however, in the years before few but the old-timers moved over desert trails.

Le Moigne's return to his Death Valley mine did not last long. He told his partner one day that he was not feeling well. Stewart advised him to go 'outside' to a doctor. Le Moigne hitched up his burro team and started for Furnace Creek. He never arrived. Later, on the old road between Stovepipe Wells and Salt Creek Le Moigne's body was found curled under a mesquite bush. Evidently he was taken suddenly ill. He had halted and set the brake; the burros could not pull away, and died with him.

Today the USGS quadrangle maps carry a notation "Le Moigne Grave." It is on the old trail, now a jeep road.

The tales about Le Moigne are numerous. 'Cap' is credited with hitching himself with a burro to produce a team when he lived down by Bicycle Lake. One of his animals was ill and, rather than wait to break in a wild one, Le Moigne just cast himself as a temporary replacement.

Another good Le Moigne yarn was told by Stewart. It seems a fellow learned the 'bank' was for sale. He had seen some of that rich ore and offered $10,000 cash. Much to his partner's disgust, Jean turned down the offer, not because the price was not right, but because the money was in the form of a check. Old Cap just didn't trust banks, and anyway the nearest one was way over in Lone Pine. It was too much of a trip for $10,000.

Cap was known all over the desert for his coffee. Up in Olancha, around World War I, Jim Nosser of Johannesburg asked for the recipe. "I take a hell of a lot of coffee, damn little water, and let it bile and bile and bile," said Le Moigne.

Hanaupah
the burro wore a bathrobe

PROSPECTORS of the old school knew the meaning of work, hard backbreaking work. A prime example was Alexander 'Shorty' Borden, onetime US Cavalryman who switched from chasing Pancho Villa down below the Rio Grande to hunting ore in the Death Valley region.

The No. 1 exhibit to prove the foregoing thesis consists of a road up the Panamint Range from below sea level to the 8000-foot contour on Telescope Peak. It was built by Borden, with a crowbar, pick, and his two burros. Where Shorty's road joins the west side road, below Furnace Creek, is a hand dug well — Shorty's Well — also Borden's single handed work.

Borden arrived in Death Valley early in the 1920's and put blankets down in an Emigrant Canyon cave which he enlarged, fitting the opening with a door and window. It served as a base from which he made prospecting trips that ranged from north of Ubehebe Crater south to the Avawatz Mtns. They were slow painstaking treks lasting for days or weeks, which were devoted to careful sampling of rock. On one such trip Borden became intrigued with some deserted Indian shacks grouped around a spring in Hanaupah Canyon. He learned that the shacks had been occupied by Indian draft-dodgers during World War I. Borden put down his blanket, tethered his burros, and stayed. In a shelf cave he found a little native shrine with 'charms' such as bird claws and snake rattles, each carefully protected in a bottle.

More important than the shrine however, were several outcroppings of ore he discovered. One silver prospect that appeared to carry considerable lead was given attention. It seemed to lead to an extensive vein. Borden dug out as much as his burro could pack and headed back for camp, a three-day journey. The assay reports were encouraging. He decided to develop his prospect into a mine. It would not pay, however, unless he had a road. No pack train operation would be profitable.

Others might have quit then and there – but not Shorty. The obstacles only made him more determined. A bulldozed road could have been blasted out up Hanaupah Canyon in a matter of weeks. Shorty, however, had no such equipment, nor money to hire any.

With his crowbar, pick, and two favorite burros Shorty Borden went to work on his road. In summer he packed into the little mountain oasis and worked down toward Death Valley floor. In winter he camped on the valley floor, dug his well, and pecked out the road up the canyon.

Shorty and his burros were great companions. His two favorites were Hanaupah Jack and Tule Hole. They were animals he loved so much he would spend his last dollar to buy them feed, even denying himself sufficient grub. They were the best fed and fattest members of the burro tribe in all the Panamints. Shorty thought Hanaupah Jack suffered from the cold winter nights. On one of his infrequent trips 'outside' he bought a flannel bathrobe in Lone Pine which he manipulated into a 'burro coat'. Hanaupah's fore legs were worked into the sleeves, with the main part of the robe serving as a blanket for the burro's back. The robe was secured in place by a liberal winding of rope and rawhide. To man, Hanaupah was an object of wonder – but to other burros he appeared possessed with evil spirits. The wild herd up on Harrisburg Flats would snort and gallop away in fright whenever Jack trotted up to exchange friendly greetings.

Present day road maps indicate the road from Shorty's well is open for about five miles. A map printed 20 years ago shows it to be nine miles long and terminating at Hanaupah Spring where Shorty had his mine. The United States Geological Survey topographical sheet also shows a road to the spring. To those who may wish to go there – a word of caution: those USGS crews might laugh at having to roll aside a few boulders – but few others would. The route should be a good challenge to the four-wheel drive fraternity.

Borden started on his one-man road project in September 1932. He had it completed before March 1933, after six months of ceaseless labor, labor that meant long days and no week-ends off.

Back in his cave-dwelling days at Emigrant, Shorty lived on a budget that approximated zero. He had a quanity of oatmeal which he cooked for his meals three times daily except for some welcome additions obtained in an unusual way. The hardy breed of traveler who assayed to reach Death Valley on tires was in no hurry. The road didn't permit speeds of more

than 10 or 15 miles an hour. In his cave Shorty could hear autos coming long before they rounded the bend upstream. He had a gold pan salted with pay dirt. Come afternoon he would sit by the cave door. When he heard a vehicle he would step down beside the road and appear to be panning gold. Travelers would invariably stop and inquire as to the prospects. Borden let them see for themselves the telltale streak of gold on the pan bottom. Conversation would follow and the prospector would issue a dinner invitation.

The dining was done in the cave with its ingeniously fitted interior. When the guests found out that the meal was to be oatmeal — just oatmeal -- back to the car the visitors would trot to return with an armful of canned goods. Shorty's strategy worked quite well. Fellow prospectors Jack Stewart and Bill Corcoran, in their tent some 200 feet away, would chuckle. "Shorty has caught another mess of fish," they said.

Shorty's ore samples, which averaged $24 in silver and lead after eliminating the high grade, caught the eye of Miss Katheryn Ronan, manager of Furnace Creek Inn. Shorty was encouraged by a small grubstake she provided. He sacked and piled up 40 tons of his better ore. He had an informal offer for hauling to the Tonopah & Tidewater at Shoshone. Now with his ore ready he found that even his depression period costs were far higher. It would cost him $20 a ton to get his sacked ore to the railroad. This plus rail fare meant a cost of $26.50 a ton to take $24 ore to the smelter at Salt Lake.

The ore was left neatly sacked opposite the spring. A regretful Shorty took his burros north to try new prospects in the Inyo Range. He never returned to keep up his assessment work.

There isn't any 40 tons of sacked ore up at Hanaupah Spring anymore. The 1940's brought war, soaring lead prices, and a smelter right at Bonnie Claire. One day some trucks drove up Shorty's abandoned road, and the ore was taken to that smelter.

By World War II Shorty was in his 70's. He gravitated to the Inyo County Hospital in Big Pine where he was a resident until the mid 1950's, Then he sold a prospect in the Inyos and moved to a rest home at Lone Pine. He suffered a stroke, which affected his speech, but in slowly pronounced syllables he told this writer, in January 1958, about his Hanaupah discovery and his big disappointment over being unable to market his ore profitably. No, he had never been paid by the truckers who took his ore to the smelter. He could still laugh though, over his oatmeal dinners. Shorty was a great little guy.

'Shorty' Borden

Aguerreberry
and Harrisburg

IN JUNE 1906 two prospectors were camped on the floor of Death Valley alongside an irrigation ditch. The place, now Furnace Creek Ranch, was then known as Greenland. One was little Frank 'Shorty' Harris, ever-roaming prospector. The other was a quiet, soft-spoken Basque, Pete Aguerreberry. Both were taking a breather after long ore-searching tramps into the rapidly building summer heat of the area.

Harris, as this writer heard it second hand from one of Shorty's numerous partners, proposed the two strike out for Ballarat and be there for the traditional Fourth of July celebration. Aguereberry had no immediate plans and was agreeable. They set out the morning of July 1, crossing the spongy sink south of the present Death Valley Airport over the trail which had been corduroyed in places to prevent man and burro from sinking deep into the soft crust. Then they climbed the trail up the steep east slope of the Panamints, bedding down near the trail.

The next morning the pair descended over a broad upland mesa now called Harrisburg Flats. At the mesa's north side were intrusive black hills. Harris and Aguerreberry took a course diagonally southwest, a course which in a few more miles would lead them to Wildrose Spring, Wildrose Canyon and then to the fleshpots of Ballarat.

At the base of the little hills Aguerreberry picked up a rock that intrigued him. He showed it to his companion to receive the ejaculation, "Hell! it's lousy with gold." Pete suggested a halt to stake out claims. Harris objected saying, "We'll come back and do it. If we don't get to Ballarat tomorrow night all the likker will be gone." With that, Shorty started off. Reluctantly Pete followed.

During the evening of July 3 and the following day Aguerreberry apprehensively heard a loose-tongued Harris boast of another bonanza discovery "right up there in the Panamints."

Blacksmith shop at Harrisburg

Dawn came July 5 and Pete headed back up Wildrose and on north to his discovery site. He reached the spot after dusk to find a hillside swarming with fellow prospectors. The next morning revealed that the newcomers had ignored Pete's little markers for they had staked out the land for hundreds of yards around. Pete protested. A now sobered Shorty came to his rescue and the original Aguerreberry discovery claim was restored.

The new camp was a producer from the grass roots down, at least for a time. When the population numbered in the hundreds a name was wanted. Harrisberry was proposed and voted for, but when the name reached the papers it had been shortened to Harrisburg.

The boom days came and went. For years Harrisburg and Skidoo, some 12 miles north, were rivals. Both produced gold –lots of it. Harris soon sold his claims, but not Aguerreberry. He tunneled deep into the little hills and built a cabin, blacksmith shop and storehouse nearby. For the next 35 years Pete worked his mine, installed air pumps, a baby-gauge railroad and compressed air drills. In marked contrast to the average miner's cabin, Pete Aguerreberry kept an ultra neat house. He even had lace curtains at the front windows.

The Panamint Range topped out in a ridge some five miles east of Aguerreberry's camp. There a flat-topped promontory offered an unsurpassed panoramic view of Death Valley's awesome magnificence thousands of feet below. Pete thought that others would be interested also. He accordingly scraped out a road from his mine to the lookout spot which he called 'Fine View', or sometimes 'Great View'.

About a year or two after the Death Valley National Monument was established in 1933 a distinguished visitor stopped at Aguereberry Camp and asked directions to Fine View. He told Pete there would be road signs put up and that the viewpoint turnoff would be marked.

No one could have been more surprised than Pete Aguerreberry when an Automobile Club of Southern California road sign crew came down the Emigrant Canyon road two or three months later and erected a sign at the Harrisburg turnoff. It carried an arrow pointing east and the name read 'Aguerreberry Point'. Pete's inquiring visitor of weeks before had been Phil Townsend Hanna, public relations director for the auto club. Hanna had learned of Pete's arduous road building just so his fellowman could share with him the magnificent panorama — and Hanna had appropriately felt the modest Basque miner deserved to have his name on the viewpoint. It is there today.

Greater View
wooden leg monument

ONE balmy spring evening in 1918 two well known Death Valley miners were passing time at Wildrose, then an old stage station on the way to Harrisburg and Skidoo. One was the Basque Pete Aguerreberry who owned and operated the Harrisburg mine. As noted in the preceding chapter, Pete had broken out a rough road from his camp to the 6650-foot ridge at the head of Trail Canyon, because he wanted others to enjoy the panoramic view of the great valley below. Pete, usually taciturn, surprised his friends that evening by telling of the lookout he termed either 'Fine View' or 'Great View'.

When Pete had finished another spoke up. From his cabin he had a 'greater view', he asserted. This second miner was Carl Mengel, owner of a good gold producer on the west ridge of Butte Valley. Mengel, an ever friendly chap, was a native of San Bernardino, a well educated mining engineer who had filed claims all the way from Barstow to Belmont and from Kawich to Saline Valley. Mengel's mother, of German extraction, had taught both English and German in the San Bernardino schools. Carl had gone through public school and Sturges Academy there, and then had taken engineering in Denver.

The death of an uncle up in Tulare County suddenly turned Mengel from a miner to an orange grower. The grove proved profitable but Mengel contracted tuberculosis. He sold the grove and spent two or three years "chasing health" as he termed it. Buying a buckboard, he drove up and down the Redwood Highway, taking a leisurely pace with 12 hours sleep at night and a nap during the noon hour. Eventually his team took him to Puget Sound where he found the air invigorating. For two years, Mengel operated as a commercial fisherman, then decided he was strong enough for mining once more.

He landed at Silver Peak, Nevada, promptly went to work as a miner, only to be promoted when the superintendent overheard him discussing rock structure in geological terms. A tunnel in the mine, one that had been dug along a broad vein,

CARL MENGEL
1868 — 1944

had pinched out. It intrigued Mengel. He decided an earth slippage had moved the vein to one side and he could pick it up. He and a partner were working alone in the abandoned tunnel when without warning quantities of overhead rock fell. Both ran but Mengel's leg was caught by the falling rock and he was pinned down -- while scores of other rocks cascaded down burying him. Miraculously Mengel's companion received but minor injuries and eventually wormed out of the debris.

For the next 24 hours men worked feverishly in relays to reach the imprisoned man. Doctors waiting at the mine entrance examined the seriously injured Mengel, found crushed bones and the start of infection. Few thought Mengel could live -- but live he did for another 39 years. This time the convalescent period was spent on the desert. With advancing summer he moved into the Panamints and, as he felt stronger, began some prospecting. Near the head of Anvil Spring Canyon in Butte Valley, Carl Mengel dug a prospect hole that after a few months he decided was really a mine, and a mine it proved to be until his death in 1944.

Below the mine, around a projecting butte was a spring. Mengel filed for the water and curbed the flow. With open rock flumes he diverted some of the flow to irrigate grape vines, apple and peach trees. Adjacent he built his cabin, a tasteful rustic one with a trellis of roses shading the entrance. Running water was a luxury as was a screened summer bedroom.

The view from Mengel's cabin -- Greater View -- was down Anvil Spring Canyon, across the Death Valley floor, up Jubilee and Salisberry passes, then clear over into Nevada. It is less known than Aguerreberry Point, partly so because it is remote and best reachable by a car with high road clearance.

Mengel kept lifelong friends in San Bernardino. During the 1920's he would come 'outside' two or three times a year -- generally staying at the Augustine Hotel where he loved to talk with Charley Rouse, the owner.

The 1940's saw Mengel doing less mining due to advancing age. On a visit to San Bernardino in 1944 he died. Friends arranged to have cremation. Then, after a service at Kremer Mortuary, the little urn of ashes was taken back to Death Valley. Atop Mengel Pass, 50 feet outside the Monument boundary, a round stone cairn was erected in which the urn was placed. Loving friends took Carl's wooden leg and placed it with the urn. At the monument base, cut in a slab of granite, is the inscription "Carl Mengel, 1868-1944."

Later Days
talc, lead, Epsom salts

PRECEDING chapters have offered selective chronicles of mines and mining camps of the Death Valley area. Undoubtedly there are as many more equally as colorful. For instance, Jack Keane discovered unbelievably rich ore in the Funerals, near Chloride Cliff, which started a rush immediately preceding the Bullfrog discovery. The Keane Wonder ore was so good the mine sold for $150,000 before any development was started. Some later owners claimed Keane Wonder was the true 'Lost Breyfogle'. It was not the $150,000 sale, however, but a later day 'battle' that gets top billing when old timers talk of Keane Wonder. Around 1912 J. R. Lane, Calico merchant, bought the mine and decided to haul his ore to the railroad at Rhyolite with a steam tractor. The one that Lane bought was the matriarch 'Old Dinah', originally purchased in the 1890's by Pacific Coast Borax and used to haul colemanite from Borate in the Calico Hills to the company's roaster at Marion. Retired when the Daggett & Borate narrow gauge was built, the old veteran had been shipped to Ivanpah and started north to open a 'tractor road' to the Lila C. On Stateline Pass, Dinah had blown a flue and had been left to rust.

When Carbonate was developed down near Confidence Mill, a corduroy road was built across the Amargosa Sink to Rhodes Wash. A new tractor was bought and Old Dinah bought and brought up. When Carbonate folded, Lane picked up the tractor, converted her to an oil burner and gave Death Valley its 'event of the year' for 1913 when his crew took the mechanical horse to the Keane Wonder. She made two trips to Rhyolite, again blew a flue and was abandoned alongside Daylight Pass.

Nearly 20 more years elapsed. H. W. 'Bob' Eichbaum built his toll road from Darwin over Towne Pass and down to historic Stovepipe Well, where he planned a resort. At the sand dunes Eichbaum's trucks bogged. He unloaded and built his resort which he first called Bungalow City (the present

Stove Pipe Wells Hotel). Then he scoured the valley for colorful relics which included the famous 'lost wagon' from up near Mesquite Spring. Then he turned his eye on the old tractor rusting up in Daylight Pass. Before he got it, however, the borax company, which was converting its Death Valley holdings into resorts, decided it wanted the tractor, and sent a mule team after it. The borax crew under Harry P. Gower and Eichbaum collided. The borax truck and teams were already hooked to the relic. Eichbaum parked his car sideways to block the road and threatened suit. Gower just laughed and reminded Bob that the justice of peace there was also on the borax payroll. The tractor still stands in front of Furnace Creek Ranch.

Carbonate was a camp with advanced ideas, even though it didn't last long. It boasted transplanted palm trees and a swimming pool, one that filled with sand in every windstorm.

Wingate Pass, scene of the famous 'battle', boasts a later chapter when it and Layton Canyon were given over to a monorail built to haul Epsom salts to the Trona Railway from a deposit in the hills south of the pass' top. The first motor proved to be too weak to haul loaded trailers up the grade. A heavier engine arrived. Its added weight pushed the monorail footings through the Searles Lake crusts, ending the project.

The valley's road north turns up Grapevine Canyon past Scotty's Castle to join US 95 near the former town of Bonnie Claire. Southwest of the castle there is a fork. The west branch goes to Ubehebe Crater and beyond to Racetrack Valley. Today it is a rough road best traveled by jeep or pickup, but it taps much historic mining country. Some 15 miles south of Ubehebe is a fork, 'Teakettle Junction'. The Racetrack is on the western fork, but on the way is another side road which heads west to the Ubehebe ghost town, site of a major lead operation during World War II. On south of the Racetrack, perched high on a hill, is the Lippincott lead mine and from there a rough jeep trail used to lead down into Saline Valley.

Back at Teakettle Junction the east fork heads up Lost Burro Gap and forks again. The left branch ends at the colorful Burro Spring. The right one traverses Hidden Valley, location of numerous old mines, a wild burro herd and joshua trees. The Lost Burro and the Keeler were principal mines of the area reached north of Ulida Flat. Then comes Goldbelt Spring, even today an active camp, and a graded county road which continues past Hunter Mtn., Jackass Spring and Lee Pump to eventually reach State Highway 190 near Darwin Junction.

East of the Furnace Creek resort area is the ghost town of Schwab with a few cabins remaining. Up the old T&T right of way from Death Valley Junction was a station named Leeland, and some six miles back in the hills is Lee Camp, a profitable mine sold by members of the well known and much abused Lee family of cattlemen who bore names like Philander, Meander, Salamander and Cubander. Because of the remoteness, writers of a half-century and more ago felt they could fictionalize with impunity. One was quoted by a Sacramento paper as finding 'Cub' Lee at Furnace Creek -- then called Greenland -- with a daughter 'Peanuts' and a son 'One Sock'. The yarn continued to state that Lee lived there because he had deserted the Union Army in the Civil War. It was color - but not truth. Cub Lee was caretaker at Amargosa Borax Works, south of Shoshone, some 80 miles from Greenland. He and his wife had no children. The death of his elder brother 'Phi' was in the San Bernardino County Hospital. Phi's death record indicates his younger brother, Cub, was all of 12 or 13 years old when Lee surrendered to Grant at Appomattox.

Along with the World War II boom in lead and the compulsory shut down of gold mining came more expansion in nonmetallics. In fact, interest had turned to deposits of abrasives, driller's clay and manganese even before the war. At Owl Holes there is today a sizable manganese operation. Another in Wingate Wash was not in operation earlier this year.

There are two principal fields of talc mining. Largest producer is the Grantham Mines located in Warm Spring Canyon. There are now 25 men on the payroll.

Tom Kennedy also has a sizable talc operation in the vicinity. Down near Saratoga the Pfizer Corporation has succeeded Southern California Minerals. Farther east are Western Talc and Sierra Talc. Up at Sheep Spring in the Avawatz was a lithographic stone quarry whose operation ended with the arrival of offset lithography. It is probable, however, that dollarwise the Death Valley mining is at a plateau it seldom reached in the days of the silver and gold boom camps: Today's operations are far more steady though admittedly they lack the storybook character associated with the Panamint, Bullfrog or Skidoo days.

Keane Wonder Mine

Suggested reading

The relatively brief listing of Death Valley works offered here is but a minor fraction of those available on the history and mining booms of Death Valley. The area, remote as it is, has served, through the years as a strong magnet for both prospectors and writers.

Adler, Pat – *Walker's RR Routes—1854,* La Siesta Press, 1965.

Albright, Horace – *The Story of Death Valley, Its Museum and Visitor Center,* Death Valley '49ers, 1960.

Bailey, Paul –*Walkara, Hawk of the Mountains,* Westernlore Press, 1954.

Belden, L. Burr —*Death Valley Heroine,* Inland Press, 1954.
Goodbye, Death Valley, Death Valley '49ers, 1956.
The Wade Story, Death Valley '49ers, 1957.
(with Ardis M. Walker) *Searles Lake Borax,* Death Valley '49ers, 1962 (1966 reprint by American Potash & Chemical and Stauffer Chemical Corps.)

Brown, Charles A. – see *Death Valley Tales.*

Carruthers, William – *Loafing Along Death Valley Trails,* Desert Magazine Press, 1951.

Caughey, John Walton — "Southwest from Salt Lake in 1849", *Pacific Historical Review,* 1937 (also as a separate). Included in *Far West and the Rockies,* volume II, issued by Arthur H. Clark Co., 1954.

Chalfant, W. A. – *Outposts of Civilization,* Christopher, 1928.
Death Valley, The Facts, Stanford, 1930 (seven printings).
The Story of Inyo, Stanford, 1942; Piñon Press, 1965.
Gold, Guns and Ghost Towns, Stanford, 1947.
Tales of Pioneers, Stanford, 1942.

Clements, Lydia – *Death Valley Indians,* Hollycrafters, 1954 et subs.

Clements, Thomas – *Geological Story of Death Valley,* Death Valley '49ers, 1954, et subs (four editions).

Coolidge, Dana – *Death Valley Prospectors,* Dutton, 1937.

Corle, Edwin – *Desert Country,* Duell, Sloan and Pearce, 1941.
Death Valley, Ward Ritchie, 1962.

Death Valley Tales, Death Valley '49ers (revised edition 1965). Chapters on the valley's fabulous past by James B. Nosser, John W. Hilton, L. Burr Belden, Ardis Manly Walker, Harry P. Gower, Phil Townsend Hanna, Carl I. Wheat, Arthur Woodward, R. A. Gibson, and Charles A. Brown.

De Decker, Mary – *Mines of the Eastern Sierra,* La Siesta Press, 1966.

Driskill, Earl C. – *Death Valley Scotty Rides Again,* published by the author, numerous printings 1955 to date. (Ranks along with Manly's "Death Valley in '49" and Chalfant's "Death Valley, the Facts" as an all time best seller.

Edwards, E.I. - *The Valley Whose Name is Death*, San Pasqual Press, 1940. (Contains the best bibliography of any book listed here.)
-*Freeman's, A Stage Stop on the Mojave*, La Siesta, 1964.

Ellenbecker, John G. - *The Jayhawkers of Death Valley*, privately printed, 1938.

Gibson, R.A. - see *Death Valley Tales*.

Glasscock, C.B. - *Gold in Them Hills*, Bobbs-Merrill, 1934.
- *Here's Death Valley*, Bobbs-Merrill, 1940.

Hafen, Le Roy and Ann - *Far West and the Rockies*, a fifteen volume series by the Arthur H. Clark Co., 1954-61. Vols. II and XV have diaries of Death Valley travelers of 1849.

Hanna, Phil Townsend - see *Death Valley Tales*.

Jaeger, Edmund C. - *A Naturalist's Death Valley*, Death Valley '49ers, 1957et subs. This noted author also has in print 'The California Deserts', 'Desert Wildflowers', and 'Desert Wildlife', all published by Stanford Press.

Kirk, Ruth - *Exploring Death Valley*, Stanford, 1956.

Kockler, Nicolas —*Old Harmony Borax*, Death Valley '49ers, 1962.

Lee, Bourke - *Death Valley*, Macmillan, 1930.
—*Death Valley Men*, Macmillan, 1932.

Manly, William Lewis - *Death Valley in '49*, four editions 1894 to 1949, various publishers. This is the one irreplacable work on the 1849 trek.

Myrick, David F.- *Railroads of Nevada*, 2 volumes, Howell-North Books, 1962-63. Also covers all of the Death Valley lines.

Nosser, James B. - see *Death Valley Tales*.

Putnam, George Palmer - *Death Valley and Its Country*, Duell, Sloan and Pearce, 1946.
— *Death Valley Handbook*, Duell, Sloan and Pearce, 1947.

Stephens, Lorenzo Dow – *Life Sketches of a Jayhawker*, Nolta Brothers, 1917.

Walker, Ardis Manly - *The Manly Map and the Manly Story*, Death Valley '49ers, 1954.
- *Freeman Junction*, Death Valley '49ers, 1961.
- *Searles Lake Borax*, see Belden, above.
- *Death Valley and Manly, Symbols of Destiny*, Death Valley '49ers, 1962.

Wheat, Carl I. - At the time of the 1949 Death Valley Centennial this noted historian wrote "Trailing the Forty-Niners Through Death Valley", "Forty-Niners of Death Valley, a Tentative Census", and "Pioneer Visitors to Death Valley After the Forty-Niners", all of which appeared as separates after quarterly publication.

Wheelock, Walt — *Desert Peaks Guide, Part I*, La Siesta Press, 1964.

Wilson, Neill C.- *Silver Stampede*, Macmillan, 1937.

Woodward, Arthur - *Camels and Surveyors in Death Valley*, Death Valley '49ers, 1961.
- also see *Death Valley Tales*.

Index

MINES